D1417602

You Can Be
Anything!

You Can Be Anything!

From A to Z

Sarah Montague

ViLLard • New York

Copyright © 2002 by Sarah Montague

All rights reserved under International and Pan-American Copyright Conventions. Published in the United States by Villard Books, a division of Random House, Inc., New York, and simultaneously in Canada by Random House of Canada Limited, Toronto.

VILLARD BOOKS is a registered trademark of Random House, Inc. Colophon is a trademark of Random House, Inc.

Library of Congress Cataloging-in-Publication data is available.

ISBN 0-375-50782-5

Villard Books website address: www.villard.com

Printed in the United States of America on acid-free paper

2 4 6 8 9 7 5 3

First Edition

For my mother
and the class of '87

Introduction

This is a book
about grown-ups

For grown-ups
who have grown.

This is not
for your children

But may be
suitable for
delinquent
young teens.

You Can Be Anything!

Amy is Adopted.

Her real parents didn't want her so they gave her away to go live with strangers.

Are you a good girl?!

Bill is Born Again.

He will not shut up about Jesus and the Bible, and no matter what you say he smiles and shakes his head in condescending sympathy for your poor lost soul because when he's in heaven with Jesus and the angels and all the ice cream he can eat, you will be burning in hell.

Do you Like going to Church?!

Clarence works at the Cemetery.

His fancy for dead animals as a child blossomed into a fine career working as the gravedigger and caretaker at the finest cemetery in town. It also keeps him occupied just enough to prevent him from actually becoming a serial killer!

Do you ever wonder where
dead people Live?!

Dana is a Drinker.

She used to have a lot of friends. Now she drinks cheap wine at home and annoys people by calling them at inappropriate times, slurring her words, repeating herself, and then forgetting about it the next day.

Do you Like taking sips of your parents' cocktails?!

Evan is an Engineer.

He always got straight A's in school and excelled in subjects like math and biology. Evan is usually rejected socially because of his greasy hair and thick glasses.

Do you wear glasses?!

Fiona is a failure.

Her husband left her for a younger woman. She wasn't good enough at making him happy and she wasn't pretty enough to make him stay.

Are you good enough so people won't leave you?! (I hope so!)

Glen is a Garbageman.

He dropped out of school and has a criminal record. He can only do manual labor because he has no other talent or skill. Sometimes it makes him angry to pick up the rich people's garbage, so he runs over the trash cans with his truck "on accident."

Do you Like taking out the trash?!

Hanna is a Housekeeper.

She spends her days cleaning the toilets of rich people so they don't have to. They always smile at her, but when they're not looking she steals from them.

Do you ever "borrow" things
that are not yours?!

Ian is an Inmate.

He was unable to function in a society with laws and rules. Now he has to wear an orange jumpsuit and fight with other criminals about what to watch on TV.

Do you like to break
the rules sometimes?!

Jane is a Junkie.

She's addicted to heroin. She only snorts or smokes it because she's afraid to shoot up. Sometimes she sleeps with her dealer to get more smack. He is skinny and smells bad.

Are you afraid of needles?!
(I hope so!)

Kevin is a "kicker" on a football team.

It's really a silly sort of thing for a grown man to do, isn't it? He can't really play any other position on the team because he's not fast or strong. So he just kicks.

Do you like playing football?!
(I hope you play quarterback! It's the only worthwhile position on the team!)

Luke is a Lawyer.

His parents have lots of money, so he was afforded opportunities most kids don't get, like never having to work and his parents paying for his school and rent and buying him a car, so he could join a frat house. He will always be a little better than you or me.

I hope you have really
rich parents!

Micah is a Dungeons & Dragons master.

When you roll the dice he says things like "You are now entering a dark corridor. You have a magic dagger and the charisma of 9." He's never had a girlfriend.

Do you Like pLaying games?!

Ned is a narc.

Everybody hates him because he sticks his nose in people's business and then tattles to their superiors. The others would never play with him at school or invite him to parties because he even told on the cool kids.

Do you Like the cool kids?!
(Then don't bLow it!)

Owen is an Order Taker.

He won't ever move up to management or anything like that. They just keep him because he shows up on time every day. He tries to get the high school girls to hang out with him after work. He even offers to buy the beer, but most of the time they say no.

Do you like to be on time?!

Petra is a painter.

Her parents bought the tortured-genius myth and still support her while she lives in New York and does her "work." She gets to sleep in and pierce her nose and never be very responsible.

Do you like to draw?!

Quentin is a Drag Queen.

He always Liked playing dress-up and getting into Mommy's cosmetics. As a youngster he enjoyed stealing his sister's underthings and wearing them to school.

Have you ever worn anything of your sister's?! (I won't tell!)

Rita is a Receptionist.

She gossips constantly and wears revealing clothing. She doesn't really care if she gets fired for stealing stamps and pens, or for having sex in the conference room drunk after hours last week. I mean, how hard is it to get another receptionist job?!

Do you like answering the phone and playing office?!

Sasha is a schizophrenic.

She hears voices in her head and has imaginary friends. She also has several distinct personalities! Sometimes she has to be institutionalized due to erratic behavior.

Do you ever talk to yourself?!

Todd is a "Trekkie."

He's really into sci-fi and actually dresses up like Spock at Star Trek conventions. He says things like "Chakotay and Borg at Wolf 359 taking out a shuttle" and "Lwaxana is in the Romulan quadrant!" He's a virgin.

Do you Like TV?!

Ursula is an undesirable.

She slept around a lot during high school because she was an early bloomer suffering from low self-esteem. Now she's always the last person at the party asking, "Hey, where's everybody going?"

Do you hate it when parties end?!

Vicky is on Valium.

She has a hard time functioning without the help of her medication. She goes to the country club and organizes charity events, but inside she knows her whole marriage is a farce and can't believe her husband for one minute thinks she doesn't know he's sleeping with his secretary.

Does your daddy have a
pretty secretary?!

Warren is a weasel.

His father never paid full price for anything, and neither will he. He often brags about the "great deals" he gets by manipulating and cheating others. He has beady eyes.

Do you ever cheat?!
Just a Little?!

Xebon Likes X-rated magazines.

When he was fourteen he found some at the bottom of his dad's toolbox in the garage. Now he hides them from his wife behind the hot water heater in the basement!

Do you Like finding
hidden treasures?!

Yolanda is a Young Republican.

She comes from a wealthy family and never had to lift a finger to support herself and has never really had a real job. She annoys her friends by spouting off all this preachy stuff about the economy and cutting out welfare.

Are you on welfare?!

Zeke is a Zookeeper.

He works forty hours plus overtime at the zoo. He is very quiet and keeps to himself. He thinks the animals speak to him in a secret language. Like when the monkeys throw their feces, they might be saying, "Zeke, we like you best!"

Do you Like animaLs?!

Acknowledgments

Thank you to Jennifer Rudolph-Walsh and Cara Stein at William Morris. Thank you to Bruce Tracy, for being so much more than slightly fabulous, and to Katie Zug and Xanthe and all of the remarkable staff at Villard.

Special thanks to the secret super powers of Karen Kehela and Sara Demenkoff.

Thank you to Silke for the inspiration to write this.

To Renée and Craig Snyder - 11 love!

About the Author

SARAH MONTAGUE is a native Californian. She currently lives in New York. She does not know how to cook.